written by Gary Bower | illustrated by Barbara Chotiner

A Patch on the Peak of Ararat

TYNDALE
KIDS

Tyndale House Publishers, Inc.
Carol Stream, IL

To Thatcher, Avree, Lucy, and Gemma

Visit Tyndale's website for kids at www.tyndale.com/kids.

Visit Gary Bower online at www.bowerarts.com.

TYNDALE is a registered trademark of Tyndale House Publishers, Inc. The Tyndale Kids logo is a trademark of Tyndale House Publishers, Inc.

A Patch on the Peak of Ararat

Designed by Jacqueline L. Nuñez

Edited by Sarah Rubio

Scripture quotations are taken from the *Holy Bible*, New Living Translation, copyright © 1996, 2004, 2015 by Tyndale House Foundation. Used by permission of Tyndale House Publishers, Inc., Carol Stream, Illinois 60188. All rights reserved.

For manufacturing information regarding this product, please call 1 800 323-9400.

Library of Congress Cataloging-in-Publication Data
Names: Bower, Gary, date, author.
Title: A patch on the peak of Ararat / Gary Bower.
Description: Carol Stream, Illinois : Tyndale House Publishers, [2017] |
    Series: The faith that God built | Audience: Ages 4–7. | Audience: K to
    grade 3.
Identifiers: LCCN 2016010620 | ISBN 9781496417442 (hc)
Subjects: LCSH: Noah (Biblical figure)--Juvenile literature. | Noah's
    ark--Juvenile literature. | Bible stories, English. | Ararat, Mount
    (Turkey)--Juvenile literature.
Classification: LCC BS580.N6 B68 2017 | DDC 222.1109505--dc23 LC record available at https://lccn.loc.gov/2016010620

Printed in China

23	22	21	20	19	18	17
7	6	5	4	3	2	1

This is **the peak of Ararat.**

This is **the ark that proceeded to park**
on a patch on **the peak of Ararat.**

This is **old Noah, a virtuous man,** who carefully followed God's carpentry plan By building **an ark that proceeded to park** on a patch on **the peak of Ararat.**

These are **three sons, hard-hammering guys,**
who worked with their sweethearts while watching the skies.

They helped **Mr. Noah, a virtuous man,**
who carefully followed God's carpentry plan
By building **an ark that proceeded to park**
on a patch on **the peak of Ararat.**

This is **the door up the rackety ramp** the animals climbed so they wouldn't get damp,
Built by **three sons, hard-hammering guys,** who worked with their sweethearts while watching the skies,

11

And **old Mr. Noah, a virtuous man,**
who carefully followed God's carpentry plan

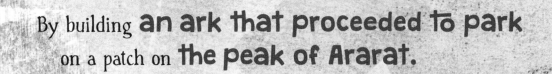

By building **an ark that proceeded to park** on a patch on **the peak of Ararat.**

These are **the animals, each in a pair**—bighorn and buffalo, beaver and bear—
Who went through **the door up the rackety ramp** the animals climbed so they wouldn't get damp,

15

Built by **three sons, hard-hammering guys,** who worked with their sweethearts while watching the skies, And **old Mr. Noah, a virtuous man,** who carefully followed God's carpentry plan By building **an ark that proceeded to park** on a patch on **the Peak of Ararat.**

16

17

This is **the water that rained with the rush** of a deafening downpour and gurgling gush

And lifted the ark and **each animal pair**—
hamster and hippo, hyena and hare—

19

Who went through **the door up the rackety ramp** the animals climbed so they wouldn't get damp,

Built by **three sons, hard-hammering guys,** who worked with their sweethearts while watching the skies, And **old Mr. Noah, a virtuous man,** who carefully followed God's carpentry plan By building **an ark that proceeded to park** on a patch on **the peak of Ararat.**

This is **the dove that brought Noah a twig.**
He joyfully jumped with a jangly jig
After **the water had rained with the rush** of a
deafening downpour and gurgling gush

23

And lifted the ark and **each animal pair**–

  lion and lioness, stallion and mare–

Who went through **the door up the rackety ramp**

  the animals climbed so they wouldn't get damp,

Built by **three sons, hard-hammering guys,**

  who worked with their sweethearts while watching the skies,

And **old Mr. Noah, a virtuous man,** who carefully

  followed God's carpentry plan

By building **an ark that proceeded to park** on a

  patch on **the peak of Ararat.**

This is **the Book of God's promise to men,**
a rainbow to say He won't do this again,
After **the dove had brought Noah a twig,**
and he joyfully jumped with a jangly jig

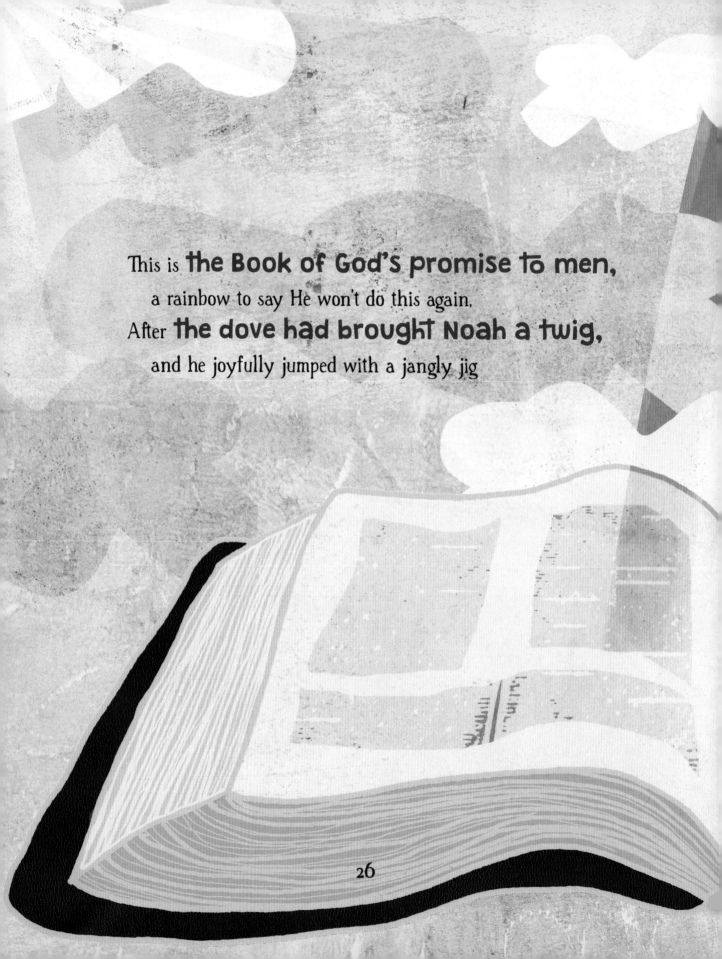

After **the water had rained with the rush**
of a deafening downpour and gurgling gush
And lifted the ark and **each animal pair**—the beasts
of the field and the birds of the air—
Who went through **the door up the rackety ramp**
the animals climbed so they wouldn't get damp,
Built by **three sons, hard-hammering guys,**
who worked with their sweethearts while watching the skies,
And **old Mr. Noah, a virtuous man,** who carefully
followed God's carpentry plan
By building **an ark that proceeded to park**
on a patch on the **peak of Ararat.**

For the whole story,
see Genesis 6–9.

When I see the rainbow in
the clouds, I will remember
the eternal covenant between
God and every living creature
on earth.

GENESIS 9:16